C O N T E N T S

Copyright is something about which people are either
terrified or totally unconcerned. There are few 'in between'
attitudes. This book will help you understand why neither
approach is valid or necessary. By Saturday night you will
have a basic understanding of why copyright exists at all, the
way the law deals with it, how to manage it as both an owner
and user, and some of the complexities of the world of
emails, intranets, websites and even CDs and DVDs. You will
also get a quick guide to the necessary jargon of the topic.
This is not a legal textbook and when any copyright issue
looks like getting out of hand it is best to consult a specialist.
Be warned that most lawyers do not handle much copyright
work so you will need more than the high street solicitor.

The basic aim of the book is not to give you all the answers
but to help you identify the questions. These questions may
turn out to be very simple but the answers rarely are. If
nothing else, you will know when a copyright issue might
arise and in that you will be ten jumps ahead of most other
managers.

Copyright is really about knowledge and we are rapidly
becoming a knowledge-based economy so a basic
understanding of what it is all about is going to be crucial for
managers in the 21st century. Those who fail to grasp this
nettle, however prickly it may seem, will be at a permanent
disadvantage in relation to those who do.

Recently I went into a tea shop in a small market town. As I
admired the rather striking modernistic wallpaper, I also
noticed that the borders round the menu were of exactly the
same pattern. In fact the tea shop owner had taken some of
the wallpaper and copied it on a high quality photocopy

machine to make the borders. She could see nothing wrong with this seemingly trivial action but I had to tell her she had infringed someone's copyright and was technically liable.

As you go through this book you will realize just how all-pervasive copyright is and how often we are all guilty of infringing someone else's rights. At the same time you may wake up to the abuse to which your own rights are so often subjected mostly, but not entirely, through ignorance.

What is copyright?

We are going to start by understanding just what copyright really is and where it fits with other similar ideas in the world of invention or creativity. We shall learn how to qualify for it and the scope of its coverage. Some basic jargon will be unraveled. Understanding copyright is not as easy as it sounds because you cannot see, hear or feel 'a copyright'. Nevertheless it is legally a piece of property just like a house, a car or a packet of cornflakes. This means it may have considerable value and can be traded in the same way as other property.

Copyright is part of a family of 'intellectual property' rights which protect the creative/inventive side of human nature. The main categories protect different kinds of inventiveness:

- Copyright – protects anything we create using our imagination or intelligence and expressed in any way
- Trade marks – guarantee who manufactures a product
- Service marks – guarantee who provides a service (banking, insurance, computer services)
- Patents – protect mechanisms, processes and machinery.

These different types of intellectual property work in different ways. This book will concentrate on copyright only.

Some jargon translated

The real problem with the language of copyright is that it does not use 'special' words but rather everyday words with special meanings. Some examples will help to explain this.

In copyright terms, whatever we create is called a 'work' whether it is a book, magazine article, painting, photograph, song or radio broadcast.

Copyright is never said to 'exist' – it always 'subsists'. The reason for this is explained in more detail under 'Where to get copyright'.

In copyright terms, people who create things are usually called 'authors' even if they are really painters, sculptors, photographers, composers, or producers of films.

The idea behind copyright

First, a little philosophy. When we create something, we do two things: we put something of ourselves into it and we become vulnerable to the outside world. Let's say you paint a picture and show it to someone. They may laugh at your efforts, criticize your brushwork or say it is inspirational. Whatever the reaction, you will take it personally as either praise or criticism of yourself, not just of your artwork. This is just as true of an internal memo in the company or a scientific paper in a journal. You may have had a brilliant flash of insight into a real problem or simply made a fool of yourself by misunderstanding the company approach or the scientific evidence.

It follows that what we create we should also control. From this comes the idea of copyright because the action we want to control is *copying* our work, whatever form that copying may take. The need to control may be because we are worried that someone will alter our work in some way or because they may deprive us of some money. It is important to realize that the copyright is quite separate from the work in which it subsists. We shall discuss this in more detail on Tuesday. The fact that you buy a book does not give you any control over the copyright in the book. Let's go back to the painting.

The painting you painted may be a good one and could sell for quite a lot of money. So you will want to control what happens to the actual painting and also what people do with it. Hanging it on the living room wall is OK but what if they want to make postcards of it and sell them in the local gift shop? You will probably feel this is unfair and they are making money out of your ability to paint.

Different rights

Copyright falls into two quite different parts: moral rights and economic rights.

Moral rights
So, as an artist, you have two quite different ways of looking at your painting. Firstly, you will want to make sure that

nobody messes about with it by changing it and you will also want to make sure it has your name on it when it is put in any sort of exhibition. You certainly will not want someone else's name on it. There is the other side to this problem too. You may gain a reputation as an artist and so not want other people's paintings sold or exhibited as if they were your work. They might be lousy paintings and this will damage your reputation as well as deceiving the general public. These rights are called 'moral rights' because they have nothing to do with money or reward but are about protecting the 'self' in the painting that you put there when you painted it. We shall return to moral rights on Thursday.

Moral rights give the author the right to:

- be named as the author
- prevent the work being changed significantly
- prevent the work being added to
- prevent anything significant being taken out of the work
- forbid anyone else being named as the author

- prevent their name being added to something they did not create.

Economic rights
To be honest, most people are at least as interested in what their property is worth as anything else. So copyright also offers a way of protecting a work so that the author can have a chance to exploit it by managing the way it is used in a market-place environment. It is the economic value of what we create that really concerns most of us. And this is where copyright really comes into its own. As a property right, the owner of copyright has a product that may be worth a few pennies or several million pounds. Copyright gives that author the exclusive right to manage the way it is sold, hired, licensed or generally made available to the public.

Object and copyright are different

The value of the copyright in a work may have nothing to do with the value of the work itself. For example, let's assume that painting is of the local village green. The painting may be fairly unremarkable when viewed by an art critic but could be the only record of the village green at a particular time and so would be very valuable to the local community. That local community may wish to produce postcards from the painting or reproduce it in a Millennium celebration of the village or even put on T-shirts. All of these activities make the painting a valuable asset to be used in different ways. The artist may get far more from allowing the painting to be used for the promotion of the village than would ever be realized if the painting were sold at auction.

The rights that authors have include:

- copying
- distributing including renting and lending
- performing, playing and broadcasting
- adapting and translating.

A bundle of rights

We have said that rights fall mainly under 'moral' or 'economic' headings. When we think about the painting we now realize that the artist has a lot of different rights in it. Although these are usually put under the umbrella of 'copyright' there are quite a lot of different types. But if you take the definition of 'author' as anyone who creates something then this brings in lots of other groups as well. For example, a ballet dancer is creative, so is a pop artist, as they both interpret the music in their own way. If they did not do that we would all be satisfied with watching or listening to robots. So performers get rights in their performances just like other authors and these are called 'rights in performance'. Performers get a rather different set of rights because of the nature of what they do.

Performers have the right to stop other people:

- recording their performance
- broadcasting the performance
- changing the recording of a performance.

Take a look at a typical CD on your shelf at home. It consists of a sleeve, perhaps some notes on the music, the disc itself, 15 different tracks each of which is from a different composer and performed by a different singer. Some of the tracks have a backing group. Some are vocal and some are just instrumental. That one disc could have more than 60 different copyrights. Composers, singers, instrumentalists, cover designers, note writers – all have rights.

We can now see that something as commonplace as a CD or amateur pantomime at Christmas can actually be a very complex work from a copyright point of view.

Where to get copyright

No life of its own

By now you can see that, in one sense, copyright does not exist at all. Although it is a right which authors have, you cannot actually show it exists. For this reason copyright is described as 'subsisting' rather than 'existing'. All this means is that 'exist' implies that something has a life of its own. Whether or not anyone is there to see it, a palm tree on a desert island still exists. Well, some schools of philosophy do argue otherwise, but that should not bother us just now. Copyright only has a life of its own as part of something else, so it 'subsists' (it is underneath something else).

To qualify

Not everything qualifies for copyright. There are three tests which have to be applied in order to claim something is copyright:

- it must be original
- it must be fixed
- the author must be a person who qualifies.

We shall look at each of these in turn to see what they actually mean.

Original

Copyright is there to give some kind of protection when
something new has been thought up and expressed.
Therefore the work has to be original to qualify for
protection. You do not get any copyright for merely copying
something else or producing something so commonplace and
ordinary that anyone could have thought of it. If you draw a
map for someone to find the local pub, it may be so
rudimentary that it could not justify the label 'original' but to
draw a quick sketch of what the pub looks like could. It all
depends on the amount of skill, labour and effort that has
been used to create the drawing.

The real test is to ask if what you did was your own work.
For example, to make a photograph of an existing
photograph would not really count as anything new. But if
two people went walking in the countryside and both stood
in exactly the same place and took a photograph of exactly
the same view, they would both be able to claim copyright in
their photograph even though the two were virtually
identical. No copying had taken place and each person had
used their own skill and knowledge (as well as their own
camera) to take the photograph.

To take something that already exists and merely make a few
minor changes will not create a new copyright work. Making
major changes probably will, but in the process it is almost
certain that the copyright of the author of the original work
will have been infringed, so this is not a good way to obtain
copyright in anything.

Fixed

Copyright is essentially about copying something therefore it follows that for something to be copyable it must exist for long enough for copying to take place. We shall meet this problem again on Thursday. A good example is an after-dinner speech. The speaker does not have a written text but works from a few notes, long experience and memory. The speech actually delivered is unique but is not copyright because it is not recorded. It goes from speaker to listener and is immediately lost. Therefore it cannot be copyright because it could not be copied, neither could the speaker prove that what he or she said had been copied.

It would all be different if someone hid a tape-recorder under the table. Even if the speaker did not wish the speech to be recorded, it would still become a copyright work because it had been fixed on tape. The real importance of this rule is that if you simply tell someone you have a good idea, whether for a new management technique, a new piece of machinery or the plot of a whodunit, there is nothing to stop them taking that idea and using it themselves. So the golden rule is: always write it down.

Qualified person

Not quite everyone who creates something is qualified to claim copyright although those who cannot are getting fewer and fewer as time goes by. The essential qualification is not age, status or competence but nationality. Copyright is a national business. Each country has its own laws, but most belong to one or more major conventions on copyright protection. Essentially, these say that a national of any one country which has signed up to the conventions is protected as if they were a national of the country where they created or published the work concerned. Nationals of countries which have not signed up do not get protection unless they publish in one of the signed-up countries.

A UK citizen publishes a book of poems in Turkey and is protected by copyright there because Turkey has signed up to the relevant conventions. A national of North Korea (which has not signed up to anything) cannot claim protection for their work in the UK unless it was first published in the UK.

Copyright myths

Here are some myths to be avoided:

Copyright must be registered.

Untrue. Countries which have signed up to the major conventions on copyright are not allowed to insist on registration. Copyright is automatic on creation.

If a work does not have the copyright symbol © then it is not copyright.

Untrue. The symbol is not required in most countries to

claim copyright (although rules vary for internal legal purposes). It is a useful reminder to users that a work is protected but it is not essential.

A copy of a work must be deposited with the national library of the country concerned to claim copyright.

Untrue in most countries. A so-called 'copyright deposit' (properly called 'legal deposit') is to help a nation maintain an archive of its national published output, not protect copyright for authors and publishers.

Summary

Today has provided an overview of what copyright is all about. You now have a basic grounding in why copyright exists at all and an idea of some of the benefits it can bring. You may also begin to think about the implications of ignoring copyright altogether. This can be a serious matter for users and owners. Users can end up in court for ignoring someone else's rights and owners can lose out by failing to control their copyright and gain income from it. By keeping the basic principles in mind that we learnt today, you will be able to grapple with the issues dealt with throughout the rest of the week. Copyright is a block-building topic so it is important to follow it through methodically and constantly refer to what has gone before.

Tomorrow we shall tackle the thorny question of the law that establishes copyright and how it works.

How the law works

Today we shall learn something of how the law on copyright works in the UK. Copyright law in any country is never simple. It is always specific to the country concerned so what is said in this chapter can only be applied to the UK (excluding the Channel Islands and the Isle of Man, the former being subject to Acts passed in 1911 and 1956 and the latter having brought in its own legislation in 1992). It also applies to those few remaining dependent territories that are scattered around the world. Although many procedures and even some of the law itself may be similar in other countries, it is dangerous to interpret the law of one country by looking at that of another.

The international dimension

It may seem strange to start with the international side of copyright but this is important as most copyright products which are important in business (databases, electronic information sources, computer software, images, games) are international in character. They do not respect national borders and cross them without any formality.

People often talk of 'international copyright' but there is no such thing. What does exist is a series of international treaties which give mutual protection, as we found out yesterday when looking at who qualifies for copyright. Each country passes laws which give an accepted minimum of protection. But essentially, when you want to do anything (publish, sell, copy, broadcast, etc) the law of the country where you want to do it is the one that matters.

A researcher wanted to copy some articles from magazines. They were published in different countries – Germany, Argentina, Russia and the USA. He tried to find out the law in each country to see if it was allowed but he need not have bothered. The copying was to take place in the UK so only UK law applied.

The law in the UK

The UK Copyright Act has the dubious honour of being the longest in the world. Fortunately, much of it also deals with patents and designs which need not detain us here (although you may need to know about those as well at some point). The UK is a world leader in copyright terms, both because it has the oldest legislation in the world (an Act was passed in 1709) and because it is one of the only two net exporters of copyright material in the world (the other is the USA). This underlines just how important copyright law is. We shall now explore the labyrinth of legislation to see how it works and what are the pitfalls when trying to discover our rights and privileges.

The basic Act

The basic legislation with which everyone must begin is the
Copyright, Designs and Patents Act (CPDA) 1988. This Act
replaces one dating from 1956 which in turn replaced one
from 1911. You can be forgiven for asking why you need this
piece of history. The reason is simple: some aspects of these
two very old Acts are still current today and, although you
may not often come across them, you do need to know that
this is a possibility.

Even when you have the CPDA on your desk, you have to be
aware of a number of serious traps when trying to work out
what it means.

The traps are that the Act:

- contains language which is imprecise and needs to be
  interpreted
- has clauses which have been expanded by subsequent
  Statutory Instruments (SIs)
- has clauses which have been added by new SIs
- has clauses which have been replaced in total or part by
  other clauses in SIs
- has been interpreted by quite a lot of case law.

Until you have gone through this whole checklist to see if the
clauses relevant to your problem have been changed in any
way, you cannot be certain what the law says.

In addition, there are all sorts of transitional arrangements
when the law changed to protect the rights of intellectual
property owners. These are often hidden away in 'Schedules'
at the back of the Act and can be very complicated. They are
made worse by the legal jargon and rather stuffy grammar
used to write them.

Civil or criminal?

Generally, copyright is a civil law matter. In other words, you instruct a solicitor and go to court for a judge to decide who is right in a dispute. You also carry all the initial costs and can have these refunded by the other side if you win or have to pay theirs if you lose. Where acts of piracy happen, such as making hundreds of copies of videos to sell at car boot sales, the police may be called in as the action is similar to theft or fraud.

Dividing up the copyright world

Copyright law divides the world up into different 'classes', each with its own rules. When getting involved in copyright you need to be clear about which 'class' you are dealing with.

The different classes are:

• Text and words including plays and musical scores
• Artistic works
• Sound recordings
• Films (and videos, although the law does not mention them)
• Broadcasts

- Computer programs
- Databases
- Performances.

Any work can qualify to be in more than one class at a time, as explained on Sunday when we looked at a 'bundle of rights'. So a TV programme could also contain the words of a play, a sound recording, part of a film and have pictures of statues or paintings. The rights which we described on Sunday are also found in all of these different classes so you can build up a really complicated matrix of rights and works.

The traps

We saw earlier today that there are some traps in trying to understand the law. We are going to look at some of those traps in more detail now.

Imprecise language
There are lots of words which are undefined in the Act but which are important when the law has to be interpreted, especially by the courts.

The most important words and phrases which cause problems are:

- substantial
- reasonable
- original
- fair dealing
- librarian.

This is not a complete list but highlights some of the more important ones.

Substantial. This is important because the owner has the right to protect all or a substantial part of a work. Therefore if someone uses an insubstantial part of a work they do not do anything wrong. But why would they want to do that? One judge said 'If it's worth copying, it's worth protecting'. But there are other places in the Act where it may be an infringement if people copy things for substantially the same purpose or at substantially the same time. But it is not clear what 'substantially' means in any of these contexts.

> If you copy a couple of pages out of the middle of a 500 page novel, that *might* not be substantial; to copy the very last page of a thriller where it says it was the vicar not the butler 'whodunit' would be substantial even though the actual quantity was very small.

Reasonable. This is always a trick word in English law. You are allowed to do all kinds of things which are reasonable. In some circumstances you may copy a reasonable part. But reasonableness is never defined and is left to individual judgment which will then be tested in court if necessary.

> A judge once said that 'What is reasonable is what may be considered reasonable by the man on the Clapham omnibus'. Although this is sexist, regionalist and classist, it gives the general idea that what is reasonable will be decided on the merits of each individual case.

Original. We looked at being original on Sunday but there is very little in the way of law that helps you decide just what is original and what is not. If something was copied from somewhere else, then it cannot be original.

*Fair dealing.*This term is banded around by people but rarely understood. This is because it has no legal definition. We shall look at fair dealing in more detail on Wednesday but at the moment it is enough to say that the purposes for claiming fair dealing are set out in some detail but how much of a work you can use is not.

Librarian. You might think this is a rather specialized word to focus on but most managers use libraries (or ought to) and many firms have libraries of one sort or another. As libraries figure heavily in the Act it will be worth spending two minutes on them, again on Wednesday. But note for now that there is no definition of a 'librarian' or a 'library'.

Precise language. Although many words are used without definition, it is also important to note that many words *are* defined at the back of the Act. Some of these definitions are technical but others are ones you would never guess. For example an 'article' (when talking about a magazine) is defined as 'an item of any description'. This is both highly precise and painfully imprecise.

IT'S A WOOLY DEFINITION

The different 'classes' in copyright

The copyright world is divided up into different 'classes' depending on the type of material concerned. We now need to look at these, as the class to which a particular object belongs may not be as obvious as we would like.

Text and words
Text and words are defined as anything which is written, spoken or sung and which has been fixed in a written or other form. This class includes:

- books and magazines
- letters and other papers including unpublished letters and diaries
- words of a song or poem even if it is not written down but only recorded using a tape-recorder
- directions for a play
- the score of a musical work.

Databases
Legally a database is a separate class from text and words. The definition of a database is very broad and is given as:

'a collection of works, data or other materials which are arranged in a systematic or methodical way and are individually accessible by electronic or other means'.

If you think about it, this includes obvious things such as bibliographies, directories, lists of products, an index of railway stations or a price list, but it might also include your album of family photographs. Organize anything in a methodical way and it is likely to be a database and a separate Database Right now exists which we will learn about on Tuesday.

Artistic works

This is a very broad class which includes maps, plans, buildings, hand-made jewellery, company logos as well as the things you might expect such as pictures, photographs, prints, sculptures and drawings.

Industrial drawings

The manufacturing industry has to produce drawings to make products such as machinery. These drawings are copyright but there are special rules called Design Right if they are used to actually make something.

Sound recordings

This class includes anything which can carry a sound including vinyl discs, CDs, DVDs, wax cylinders or tape of various kinds. The copyright in the sound recording is quite separate from the content of the recording. We learnt something of this on Sunday.

Films

Films are a separate class and must consist of a series of images from which a moving image can be produced. So a CD-ROM, DVD, celluloid or nitrate film, video (although the law never mentions this word) and presumably the old seaside 'What the butler saw' type of machine are all films. But beware that a microfilm, despite its name, is a series of photographs, not a film at all.

Computer programs

It is important to remember that a computer program is

protected by copyright just like a book or magazine article. This applies whether the program is in electronic form or simply written down on paper. You also need to distinguish the program from the work it drives. A CD-ROM will contain material, such as pictures or text, which is copyright. The program that drives the search engine or loads images on the drive is quite separate and is protected by copyright as well. The law makes special provision for use of computer programs which will be discussed on Tuesday and Wednesday.

Performance
As we learnt on Sunday, performers have rights in what they perform and these performances are a separate 'class' of copyright work. As they are often highly valuable they are carefully protected.

Subsidiary legislation

The three types of SI mentioned earlier have to be consulted before a real understanding of the law can be achieved. We shall have a brief look at these different types now.

Supplementary legislation
There are many places in the basic Act where a phrase such as 'the Secretary of State may by order provide . . .' turns up and these regulations need to be found, using reference works such as *Statues in Force* or an appropriate legal database. Basically, if you find a phrase like this, then you can be sure that regulations exist as the Secretary of State (for Trade and Industry) has made regulations in every case.

These supplementary regulations can deal with all sorts of different (and unlikely) subjects including:

- what librarians (not defined) can copy
- who can make recordings of broadcasts
- what constitutes an educational establishment
- copying of folksongs
- management of licensing schemes
- how to mark maps copied for public inspection.

These are just examples and certainly not an exhaustive list.

Additional legislation

This is a trap which is much more difficult to avoid. The basic Act warns you that there will be regulations to find out about, but since 1988 new legislation has been passed which is difficult to detect. The safest thing is to look at the list below and, if it includes something that concerns you, then do some research to find out just what the law now says.

The most important areas where there have been changes are:

- computer programs
- databases
- how long copyright lasts
- lending and rental of copyright works.

We have already looked at the first two and we shall take a brief look at the others on Tuesday.

Case law

This is hard to track as copyright cases rarely make the headlines. They are important for understanding what words and ideas in the law might mean.

You might think that you know what a 'current event' is but two recent cases now show that 'current' may mean 'it happened a long time ago but it is still of public interest'. Rules on reporting the news have to be re-thought.

Summary

Today we have learnt a lot about how the law in the UK works. It cannot be taken at face value and needs a lot of research to interpret it in some areas. Words and phrases do not necessarily have the same meaning as in ordinary speech and trying to find out what recent legislation says or how the courts have interpreted it can be complicated. The copyright world is divided up into different classes. Having discovered how the law works, tomorrow we shall find out just what this means for those who own copyright and the implications for business and industry as well as the public sector.

Authors and owners

Today we are going to look at how copyright is created, but we will spend most of the day exploring who owns it and what can be done with it. As copyright is a property, this has considerable economic and business implications. As these are often overlooked in many businesses, today should be of particular value in helping managers to identify potential sources of income and a potentially valuable piece of property.

Creating copyright

On Sunday we learnt that copyright has no life of its own but it is still a property right the same as any other type of property. However, it has to be created by someone in the first place. That someone, called the 'author', has a very limited role in UK law. They do have certain limited 'moral' rights, as discussed on Sunday, but otherwise the author has only one major role to play and that is fixing how long copyright lasts.

Who is the author?

It is fairly obvious that the author is the person who creates the work. The person who writes the book or magazine article, paints the picture, takes the photograph, composes the music, writes the software program or designs the house is the author. These are fairly obvious. But what about other types of material? Sometimes there is just no one clear person who created the work at all.

How would you define the author of a film or a CD?
With the bundle of rights we explored on Sunday, can
we say who is the author? Not really. So the law makes
special rules for works like these but they have little
impact on reality. The author of a film is the producer
but we shall see that this does not mean much in
practice.

The importance of the author

Authors have two important roles in UK law:

- their nationality helps decide if the work is protected by
  copyright law at all
- the date of their death fixes how long copyright lasts.

We talked about the question of nationality on Monday
when we looked at how international law works. The
cheerful question of when the author died is far more
significant.

Death of the author
Most intellectual property rights are limited in some way by
time. Patents can be renewed for a limited period but then
run out; trademarks can last for as long as they are used and
re-registered. But copyright has a limited lifespan and its
length is fixed by the date of the death of the author.
The rules are very complex in some areas but a rule of
thumb will keep you on the straight and narrow. Basically,
copyright expires 70 years from the end of the year in
which the author died. Copyright always runs out on
31 December, never mind the exact date the author
died.

For example, an author dies on 10 January 1990 so copyright will expire on 31 December 2060. If another author dies on 30 December 1990, copyright will still expire on 31 December 2060. So one author gets just 70 years from death while the other gets nearly 71 years. It may be rough justice but it makes life simpler when trying to work out when copyright expires.

No author
Not every work has an author. A quick look round your desk or company library will reveal many works without authors.

A manager in an engineering works may have on the desk the company annual report, statistics on wages and salaries from the DfES, standards on metal fatigue issued by the British Standards Institution, a press release from a rival manufacturer and a disk containing software to update the PC in the corner. Most of these items will have no personal author.

73095

In these cases the law decides that copyright lasts for 70 years from when the work was published as no human author has any real interest in it.

Government publications
Copyright in 'Crown' publications is different. Basically, anything put out by Government is protected for 50 years from when it is published, without any reference to when or if the author died. But, as we shall see on Friday, a lot of government material is much more freely available.

Owning and acquiring copyright

We have sorted out in general terms how long copyright lasts but that is often of little interest except in historical or academic circles. The key question is: who owns copyright?

Remember that copyright is a property and a tradable commodity. Therefore it has value and it is this that makes the question of ownership so important. It can be left by people as part of their estate, sold or leased in whole or in part. Equally you can buy or lease it in the same way.

The royalties on the online kareoke industry in Japan in 1997 were over $300,000,000 so do not underestimate the value of the product we are discussing. Authors of novels sometimes get up to £250,000 advance on sales of their books.

First ownership
Not surprisingly the law says that the first owner of copyright is the author. After all, if the author created the work, presumably the author ought to own it. Although that is the basic rule, there are one or two important exceptions.

You might be excused for asking that, if the author is the first owner, why did we learn earlier that the author was of limited importance. The reason is quite simply that the more important person is the owner, so when the author is also the owner then the author is important *as the owner*.

Employees

Although the law gives first ownership to authors, managers need to be aware that this is not the case when employees create something as part of their employment. In this case, the employer owns the copyright. But this is true only if the work is created in the course of employment.

A scientist working at a research station in the countryside prepares a scientific report on genetically-modified cabbages. This is what she is employed to do, so the copyright belongs to the research station. The same scientist is also a keen ornithologist and spends lunchtimes carrying out a census of birds visiting the site. She then publishes this in the proceedings of the local natural history society. As it is not her job to study birds, she will own the copyright and be free to publish the article anywhere she wishes. Unless, of course, it breaches some security rule which would be a different issue.

Despite being owned by the employer, how long copyright lasts is still fixed by when the employee dies. This does not apply to employees in the civil service (the Crown).

Works that are commissioned
Special care needs to be taken when you commission someone to create something for your company or yourself. In 1989 the law changed from giving the copyright to the person who commissioned the work to the person who creates the work. This makes a considerable difference and has serious implications for the financial aspects of contracts with other organizations and companies. A simple and true example from family life will make it clear how important this can be (only the names have been changed to protect the innocent):

John and Jane got married and asked a commercial photographer to come and take photos of the wedding. They received the album to choose the photos they wanted but were unwilling to pay for extras for relatives, best man, bridesmaids, etc. They took them to a copyshop with a high quality copier and made quite a lot of copies. Unfortunately for them, the photographer came in at that moment and made them stop. He pointed out that they owned the photos they bought in the album but not the copyright in them. If they wanted more copies they had to pay for them. That is how the photographer makes his money.

Get your contract right
The same is true of a company commissioning someone to

carry out research, take photos of the site, prepare a logo or publicity material. You only get what you contract and pay for. If you ask someone to design a logo for use on *notepaper* then you have the right to use the logo in that way but if you want to put it on your website you may find they will refuse to let you unless you pay a further fee. If you do it without their agreement, you may end up in court, which is what happened to a no-longer famous telephone company.

Equally, if your organization agrees to create something for someone else, make sure everyone knows what they are getting and put a proper price on each separate use of whatever it is you create.

Make sure that all such contracts are in writing. The law requires that copyright is transferred *in writing* so mere 'understandings' will not do.

Owners' rights

But just what rights do owners have that they can trade in this way? The basic answer is 'Quite a lot' so do not underestimate the value of what you create or what others create for you.

It is important to realize that the law starts by giving owners certain exclusive rights. Tomorrow we shall see how those are modified to help users. Exactly what these rights are will differ from one 'class' of material to another.

Copying
Obviously, owners have the right to copy a work, which is where the word 'copyright' comes from. But copying is not

simply making a photocopy of a text. It covers all kinds of other things you might want to do as well.

Copying includes:

- reproducing the work in any form
- storing a work in a computer
- making a 3D work of a picture or painting, for example taking a photograph of a 3D object such as a statue
- making transient or incidental copies of any work, for example by sending them by fax.

Publishing and distribution
Once you own copyright, you have the right to publish the work or authorize anyone else to publish it. This can include carving up the rights to publish any way you want. Popular authors often sell hardback rights to one publisher, paperback rights to another and keep film and TV rights for themselves. They can also sell rights for limited periods (for example hardback in North America for five years but paperback rights for ten years).

Performing, playing or showing
The owner has the right to control all of these actions so the author of a play or piece of music can authorize or prevent its performance in public, and owners of rights in sound recordings, films and videos can stop them being played or shown in public. You may think this has nothing to do with being a manager but we shall see on Friday that staff restaurants, social clubs and even telephone 'on-hold' music systems all have problems.

Broadcasting
Including any work in a broadcast (which includes cable, satellite and perhaps websites (but wait for Thursday to discuss that)) is something only the owner can authorize. This could include reading parts of a company report on a local radio station interview, including design work prepared for the company in a TV programmme, or even just showing a camera crew round, showing off the company's achievements.

Adaptation or translation
Owners have the right to authorize the adaptation of a work. This can include the obvious one of turning a story into a play but it also includes making a strip cartoon from the plot of a book. Beware of using popular material in this way for staff magazines or publicity. In the same way, translation includes changing something from one computer program to another but also making an English translation of an article in another language.

Extraction and re-utilization
If you own the rights in a database (called Database Right

rather than copyright) then you can prevent anyone else
taking significant amounts of information from that database
and using it for their own purposes.

> If you prepare a trade directory and list all the ice-
> cream makers in town then nobody else can use that
> information to make their own directory or listing. They
> can copy down the addresses of ice-cream makers to
> write to them or phone them up but they must not take
> the list and reproduce it in another directory.

This does not stop someone else making their own list of ice-
cream makers from scratch and going into competition with
your directory. They have got to invest the time, money and
resources to do it, just as you did, not ride on your back.

Rights in performance
These are different from 'performing rights'. A copyright
owner has the right to license someone to perform the work.
When it is performed, the artist performing it then has a right
in the performance he or she gave. These performances must
not be recorded or broadcast by anyone without the artist's
permission.

> Theatres and clubs often forbid the use of camcorders
> and similar equipment during performances, even if it is
> Shakespeare or a songwriter long since dead. This is
> because the actors or singers have rights in the
> performances they give, whether or not the work
> performed is in or out of copyright.

Proving ownership

Given that copyright is a valuable commodity, it is important that everyone knows who owns it. As there is no registration process, the presumption in law is that if a work has a name on it then that person or organization is the owner. If a dispute arises over copyright the courts will assume the owner is the person who says they are the owner and anyone claiming otherwise would have to prove it. Although the symbol © has no legal status it is useful to remind people that copyright exists and also as a shorthand to say who owns it. '© Anybros Banking Services 1999' alerts other people that Anybros have rights in the work which they will defend.

If someone wants to show they wrote something at a particular time, a simple method is to make a copy of the original, put it in a sealed envelope, have this witnessed across the seal and post it to themselves. They should keep it sealed and only use it if they are challenged. This is useful for authors sending manuscripts to publishers and for musical composers too.

Remember that ideas are not protected by copyright, only the way they are expressed.

Chris has an idea for designing a new widget but does not write it down. At a party for important customers he has one glass too many and tells someone from a rival company all about the idea. The rival then produces drawings for the widget based on Chris's idea. There is no come-back for Chris because the idea was not written down (fixed) anywhere. Perhaps copyright and drink do not mix?

Summary

We have learnt that the author is vital in creating copyright works but, after that, their only real contribution to the process is their date of death which starts the copyright clock ticking. Owners (who may also be authors) enjoy a whole range of exclusive rights which are defined in law. These rights often have an effect on all kinds of activity, not just business and industry. Because copyright is a property, and often a very valuable one, it is important to write contracts properly when you buy something in as well as provide something to someone else. It is sensible to take precautions to show that you own copyright in particular works and that everyone knows who owns what.

Tomorrow we shall see how it is still possible to use copyright works in certain circumstances even though the owner has the exclusive rights we have just discussed.

Using copyright material

Yesterday we learned that copyright law gives the owner certain exclusive rights. On the face of it, this would stop anyone using that work in any way at all. But this is plainly not how the system works. We are all what we are because we have used someone else's copyright works at school, college, university or in business or for leisure.

Limiting owners' rights

People enjoy all kinds of rights but these are usually limited in various ways for the benefit of society as a whole. You may own your house and garden but you cannot build a factory on it without permission as it may cause distress to the other residents of your street. Similarly, the exclusive rights granted under copyright are, in turn, limited in various ways to make sure nothing is locked away for ever so that it cannot be used.

The three main ways in which copyright is limited are:

- Quantity – anyone can use less than a 'substantial' part of any work. Beware that 'substantial' is one of those elastic words we looked at on Monday, the exact meaning of which can only be decided in each case.
- Time – the '70 year rule' outlined on Tuesday
- Purpose – a very complex area and the main subject for us today.

The purposes for which copyright materials can be lawfully used are set out in the Act. It is very important to remember that the law starts from the assumption that each owner has exclusive rights. It then goes on to list specific areas where those rights are limited (called 'exceptions'). Statements like 'The law doesn't say I can't do it' are wrong because you cannot do anything with a copyright work unless the law says you *can*.

The main purposes where owners' rights are limited are:

- research and private study
- criticizing or reviewing
- reporting current events
- education
- library functions
- justice and democracy
- national security.

The first three reasons are grouped under a general term 'fair dealing'. We saw on Monday that this term is not defined in law. You may use some works in different ways for research, criticizing, or reporting the news, provided you think the use is 'fair'. But what is fair is left to you to decide and the owner to disagree if necessary. Fairness relates to how much of a work is used and whether the owner has lost out financially or in any other way because of the way you used the work.

John is doing local history research. He finds a book in the local public reference library published in the 1940s which he cannot take home. The publisher disappeared years ago and he cannot find the author. He makes a copy of the whole book to take home. Jennifer is studying biomechanics in the local university and sees a recent book on the topic in the same library. She decides to make a copy of it to take home rather than

buy her own which would have been very expensive.
Same action but one is fair and one not. It is obvious
which is which.

Now we can look at the different uses the law allows. On
Monday we learned that there are different 'classes' of work
and this is important now.

Research and private study
You can copy a work for non-commercial research purposes
or for private study but this does not apply to sound
recordings or films (and videos), broadcasts or computer
programs. The use must be 'fair' (see above) but for printed
works it is usually said that an article from a magazine or a
chapter of a book would usually be seen as 'fair', however
there are no hard and fast rules. If you work in industry and
commerce, note that 'research' is now limited to non-
commercial research, and users must decide for themselves
on each occasion if their use is 'commercial' or purely
academic. Note that copying for use in a study group is
outside 'private' study and may need a licence (more of this
on Friday).

HOLIDAY READING

The law does allow what it calls 'time-shifting'. It is a sort of fair dealing which allows you to record radio and TV programmes so you can watch or listen to them later on because you are out or they clash with something else you want to see or hear. [Actually this is law being realistic: you cannot stop people taping *Coronation Street* or *Blind Date* so why have a law that says it is illegal?]

Criticism or review

To be able to criticize a play, book, picture or scientific research, you must be able to quote from it. This is allowed (with the usual question: is it fair?). If you quote so much of a work the reader does not need to read the original then that is probably not fair. The same rules apply to reviewing something for a newspaper or magazine. You must say where the quotes come from but you would do that anyway for the benefit of the reader.

Reporting current events

You can use any kind of work (except a photograph) when reporting a current event. The term 'current event' is used instead of 'news' because recently the courts have put special emphasis on the word 'current'. Basically, the idea of this exception was to allow newspapers and broadcasters room to use whatever they needed because trying to get permission when you are reporting from, say, a battlefield or the middle of famine-torn Africa is a bit difficult. The term is very broad and can be used to allow institutions to make up their own internal news bulletins and circulate them to staff. This must involve digesting the news, not just photocopying other publications. But what is 'news' has been a matter of dispute.

It can be something in the past but still current in the public eye.

A lady who received infertility treatment conceived eight babies, all of which died. She later sold her story to a newspaper. She also gave an interview to a TV company about infertility treatment. Nearly two years later, another TV company made a programme about 'cheque book journalism' and included some material from the first TV company's programme. The judge allowed this as the 'Cheque book journalism' issue was a matter of public concern even though the event itself happened two years before.

Education

The most important thing to remember for any commercial organization is that education is not training. Any copying or other use of copyright works for training will have to be paid for in some way (more of this on Friday). Education is mainly a term used for schools, colleges and universities and those other institutions which offer some form of higher education such as teaching hospitals.

This will be of interest for those working in education, whether teachers/lecturers, students or administrators. But it is also important for those who have staff who are undertaking various kinds of academic education such as managers doing MBA courses, day-release or block-release students, those taking professional examinations or subjects of personal interest for family reasons.

Copying for examinations is one special case. Anything other than sheet music for performing can be copied for setting or answering an exam question. Although not specifically stated, this is usually taken to include material in a dissertation or thesis for university purposes. The danger here is that if the thesis is then published, permission to use the copyright material would be necessary. Teachers of all kinds can also make recordings from TV and radio for use in the classroom under a special licence (more of this on Friday). In fact, the law makes it clear that all educational use should be covered by licences whenever possible and makes very limited exceptions where material is not licensed. These exceptions amount to one per cent of a work in any of the four three-month periods of the year so that a grand total of four per cent of a work could be copied in any one year. This does not apply to artistic works of any kind for which licences will always be required. The only exception is making an over-head projection of an artistic work in a book to show to a class which the publishers have said they would not regard as an infringement.

Libraries

Libraries enjoy a special position in the law and have been given certain privileges for their own benefit and the benefit of their users. The actual regulations are very complex and we do not need to spend a long time on these as we can leave them to the librarians to unravel. However, anyone using a library and certainly anyone with a library of any kind as part of their management responsibilities needs to understand the basics.

Broadly speaking, libraries are allowed to make copies of works for the following reasons only:

- to supply to the user
- to supply to another library
- to protect the original
- to replace material in another library which has been destroyed or lost.

The first two reasons apply to all libraries; the second two apply to libraries in institutions which are funded by public money (public libraries, universities, schools, hospitals, etc) or to learned societies.

Users

Any library can supply a copy of a work in its collection to any reader but there are strict conditions laid down in the law for this.

Copies may be made for readers provided that:

1 the work is a literary or musical one
2 the user wants the copy for non-commercial research or private study
3 no two people get copies of the same material
4 the user is supplied with only one article from any one issue of a magazine or a 'reasonable' part of any other sort of work
5 the user signs a legal declaration saying why the copy is wanted
6 the user pays the cost of making the copy

These conditions may seem very strict and limiting, so why not just call it 'fair dealing'? The reason is simple: fair dealing is undefined and can be challenged by any owner as to whether or not it is 'fair', but copying by libraries cannot be challenged provided these strict conditions are observed. The need to charge was put in the law to protect the public sector from carrying the cost of people asking for photocopies, but *technically* it applies in the private sector too. However, the money from this requirement does not go to the owners of the copyright but to the library, so asking someone in an industrial research unit to pay their own library for making a copy is just money going round in circles to nobody's benefit. Most private firms just ignore this provision but the author is not going to encourage you to break the law deliberately.

Copying for libraries
Libraries do not always have all that the user wants in their collections so they occasionally get copies from other libraries to add to their stock. Although any library can supply a copy, only publicly-funded libraries can put them into stock. So Anybros Chemicals can send a copy to Knowall University Library for its collection, but not the other way round. Similarly, only publicly funded libraries can make copies of works to preserve them or replace material which they once owned but which has been lost, damaged or destroyed by some means.

LIBRARY

Justice and democracy
The general view is that private property rights should not impede the proper processes of justice and democracy.

Therefore users are given fairly wide privileges to use copyright material in these areas. The law allows anyone to do whatever is necessary in four major areas:

- parliamentary proceedings
- statutory inquiries
- Royal Commissions
- court cases.

However, this is not quite the permission to do anything that it may at first appear to be.

Parliamentary proceedings

This is probably the broadest category. Anything may be done that is necessary to carry on the work of either House of Parliament. So, if there is a Select committee meeting, or a debate in either House or an MP needs some information for a debate *in the House,* then that work can be copied as necessary without formality. This does not mean that MPs and Members of the House of Lords can copy anything they like – the need has to be for the work of Parliament itself.

An MP receives a complaint from a constituency member that a nearby chemical firm is polluting a local stream. If the MP needs to investigate by asking for copies of scientific articles, these must be covered by the usual procedures (fair dealing or library privilege). However, if the same MP then needs to ask a question in the House about the chemicals concerned, copies of the same articles may be made available to the Minister answering the question to make sure that Parliament has all the facts.

Statutory inquiries and Royal Commissions
Generally speaking the rules are similar to Parliament.
Someone giving evidence to committees of this sort may
need to provide copies for everyone concerned but should
not do this unless the Chair of the inquiry or commission
orders it to be done. Just to want to bring evidence is not
enough: the person in charge has to say it is necessary.

The courts
The law simply says 'judicial proceedings' but it has been
agreed that this is too broad to be fair so a general code of
conduct has been put in place which allows anything to be
copied for a court case once the writ to hear the case has been
issued. Therefore merely preparing a case is not covered by
this exception, but once the time and date of the hearing are
fixed, copying for this would be justified. In the case of
Regulatory requirements (for example in the pharmaceutical
industry) or Patent applications, these are not legal
proceedings which must take place. They are ones which
manufacturers choose for commercial reasons and so are
excluded unless the registration is challenged in the Patent
Court or on some other grounds elsewhere.

Local Government
There are special rules which allow copyright material to be
copied when material has to be open for public inspection,
such as planning applications, electoral registers and council
papers open to the public.

National security
In most laws about private property there is a special clause
which prevents individual interests obstructing what has to
be done in the interest of the nation as a whole. This is true of

copyright law as well, but it is not a clause to be invoked lightly and relies very heavily on a strict interpretation of what makes up 'national security'.

During the Gulf War a number of libraries made up information packs on unusual medical conditions for those working with the troops in the field. Normally this would not be legal but the circumstances made it a matter of national security and it was not challenged.

Computer programs
There are special rules which allow you to make back-up copies of computer programs in case anything goes wrong with the original. You can also decompile a program in some circumstances to help you design something which needs to run on that program. You can do this only if the manufacturer won't give you the information you need.

Using copyright works for other purposes
This chapter has outlined the main reasons why you can use

someone else's copyright material without their permission. In all other circumstances, permission should be sought to use material, whether it is for teaching, training, republishing, making a film or broadcast or for advertising. Sometimes it is just not possible to find out who owns the copyright in a work – perhaps nobody does now. If you have really exhausted all possibilities, then the best thing to do is go ahead and use the work, BUT set aside in some way the amount you would have been prepared to pay if you could have found the owner. If you are then challenged this is usually sufficient to calm an owner's anger. In any case, except for very high profile owners, most people are more interested in getting the credit for a work rather than money. Tracking down owners can be hard but the following can be very helpful:

For literary and dramatic works, broadcasts and films:
Authors' Licensing and Collecting Society
Marlborough Court
14–18 Holborn
London EC1N 2LE
Tel 020 7395 0600; email alcs@alcs.co.uk

For illustrations:
Design and Artists Copyright Society
Parchment House
13 Northburgh Street
London EC1V 0AH
Tel 020 7336 8811

Summary

Although owners have exclusive rights, they are also limited for the benefit of users. 'Fair dealing' can be used to allow copying for non-commercial research or private study, reporting the news or reviewing a work; and libraries have special privileges to serve both their own needs and those of users. The law, parliament, democratic government and national security also make copying legal in some circumstances. Users need to be careful not to overstep the mark but should also exercise their privileges whenever they need to. If the use is going to be really commercial, such as advertising, then permission will be needed.

Websites, intranets, email

Yesterday we looked at what users can do with copyright that belongs to other people and on Tuesday we looked at authors and owners. Both of these issues are going to be important if we want to understand the electronic world of information.

The law and electronic information

The law actually says very little about copyright and electronic information specifically. Mostly, it is a question of trying to fit the existing law on to new situations. As the law is now about 15 years old, this can prove difficult. Lack of definitions can cause problems as we saw on Monday.

One word that *is* defined is 'copying' which is:

> 'reproducing the work in any material form. This includes storing the work in any medium by electronic means and includes making of copies which are transient or incidental'.

So, whether you are creating works or using them, remember this definition in an electronic context because websites, emails and even faxes often need more than one copy to be made in order to use them.

Websites

Whether you are making or using a website, you need to

understand just what is going on in legal terms. Some of these things are not what you expect at all, neither are many of the things we take for granted necessarily legal.

Creating a website

If you create your own website using material which you or your company have written, drawn, designed or composed, you have few problems. You may want to use some existing software to program the text and set it up properly but you are usually licensed to do this when you buy or gain access to it so don't worry too much about that, as we shall see on Friday. You will then own the copyright in the website you create and can stop anyone else using that material on their websites (or anywhere else) without your permission. It is also a good idea to say that the website is copyright and who owns it, otherwise people just use your material and then plead ignorance. If you employ someone else to design your website for you, remember what we learnt on Tuesday about ownership. Just because you pay someone to design the website it does not mean you own what they provide. Make sure your agreement with them gives you the right to use the material in any way you think may be possible in the future, not just at the moment.

There is an awful lot of material available on other people's websites which can easily be cut and pasted to make your own look better. Remember that this material is also owned by someone else and you could end up in a lot of trouble by using someone else's web material without permission. When we look at licences on Friday we shall see that there are ways that this can be done.

The home page

The home page can serve all kinds of purposes, such as:

- advertising your products
- indicating what the website contains
- links to other sites
- ownership
- conditions of use.

It should certainly give details of who owns the website to avoid the pleas of ignorance just mentioned. This also means that other people can find you to get permission to use what you have put together, which could be a valuable source of revenue if you choose to license them to do it.

Allowing use

The home page also gives you a chance to show under what conditions users can have access to your website. This is your property so you can decide . You can do this in different ways:

- simply a statement of what users can and cannot do
- a statement of what is allowed but require the user to say they agree (by clicking on an icon or square)

- show that users need to register (with or without a fee) and get a password to use the site (or part of it)
- ask for a credit card number to gain access and show the charges.

Once you have set up arrangements to let people into the website, you can then decide what you will let them do and under which conditions. These conditions can be as varied and complicated as you want or you feel are necessary for business purposes. You could:

- allow any of the material to be used in any way for any purpose with or without acknowledgement
- allow downloading or printing out for personal use only
- allow students to download and print but charge commercial organizations
- allow the material to be used by others building a website, or on an intranet but not on a website.

These are just a few examples – you can work out an almost infinite number of combinations to suit any situation. But, remember, it is your property (or your company's) and you have the right to set the terms.

Hypertext links
One of the greatest benefits of web site mechanisms is the creation of hypertext links to other web sites. This system was originally seen as totally harmless and of enormous benefit to both the user and the information provider. Unfortunately it is a case of technology developing faster than the law can cope with. When you click on the hypertext link the text which you are looking for is transmitted to your PC even though we often 'feel' as if we are taken to another website on a sort of electronic magic carpet. This means you

are not simply viewing something which exists but having it transmitted to you. This virtually amounts to broadcasting which is the right of the owner, not the user. So to create a hypertext link could amount to broadcasting a work. You could be excused for thinking that if the owner of the site you have linked to did not want a work copied, they should not have allowed the link to be built. But website owners do not know links have been created unless someone tells them. To avoid this problem, it is best to build links only to homepages or seek permission from the website owner for other types of link.

Passing off
Passing off is not really a copyright matter, but more to do with trade. However, it often involves infringements of copyright. Passing off is providing goods or services which look sufficiently like somebody else's goods or services so that the buyer or user is deceived into thinking they come from one source when they actually come from another. When you create web site links, it is important that the user is always aware of whose information is being used. If you start a search in one web site and then use a hypertext link to another, the user may think that they are still looking at the first website. Make sure there are displays, borders or icons which make it quite clear whose material is being viewed, downloaded or printed. A small icon which says something like 'copyright information available here' would be enough.

Deep links
Because of the problems with 'passing off' and also the need for users to know what they can and cannot do, it is never a good idea to build links straight into the body of another website (so-called 'deep links'). Although they might save

time, they can cause all kinds of problems for both owners and users.

Liability

If you do put someone else's copyright material up on your website, are you liable or is it the responsibility of the internet service provider (ISP)? We shall look at this in more detail on Friday.

HE'S DOING DEEP
LINKS TODAY

Using websites

Using websites is full of temptations. It is so easy to download material from a website and copy or print it out. It is just as easy to send it on to colleagues or friends. But just because something is easy to do, does not make it legal. There is a general myth going around that 'anything on the web is free of copyright'. As you can see from what we already learnt today, this is just not true. A good test for any web user is:

Imagine the website or web page you are looking at is really a piece of paper. How would you behave if it were just paper? By this stage of the week you ought to

be able to answer that question quite accurately. So
the golden rule is 'Treat all web material the same way
as you would paper material'.

People who create and own websites do so for many different
reasons and have equally differing views on what they want
other people to do with their work. So it is important to try to
understand why the material is there in the first place and this
can help you to work out what is and what is not allowed. We
shall learn more about licences and websites tomorrow but
these do not solve all your problems as a user. Where the
owner of the website has set out conditions for use you must
stick to them. However, many users do not do this which may
leave you feeling uncertain. Here are a few questions that are
worth asking if you want to use someone else's web material
for any reason. Some of these questions relate to what we
learnt on Wednesday about using copyright material generally.

1 What are the owner's intentions?
2 How much do I want to use?
3 What harm would my use of the work do?
4 Has the owner specified what I can or can't do?

What are the owner's intentions? Although it is difficult to work
out what owners always intend, there are some obvious cases
where copying material, for example, would actually please the
owner. But it would all depend on your reason for copying it.

Let's say there is an advert for Surmer swimwear on a
website which the manufacturer has put out to promote
sales of swimming trunks. If you use this to tell your

friends about this bargain, the manufacturer will be very
pleased. But if you used the same swimwear image on
your own website to promote the hotel you own in
Torquay you would be in big trouble.

Generally, anything which is put on websites to promote a
product, idea, belief or policy should be safe to use provided
that the use helps the promotion of whatever it is the owner
wants to tell you about. The problem comes when the material
is used for a different purpose. Be especially careful not to use
promotional material for different, or even opposite, causes.
Quoting your opponent's texts in a political battle could be
infringing copyright and using competitors' images for
comparative advertising ('Surmer swimsuits are good but
ours are better') is full of legal traps besides copyright.

Even where your interests are the same as the website owners,
you may find the owner still objects to use of the material. You
may be an enthusiastic environmentalist but to take pictures or
deigns from another environmental protection website and
use them on yours will still be an infringement. The original
designer may expect you to pay for the privilege, even though
you are working for the same cause.

How much do I want to use? We learnt on Wednesday that anyone can use less than a 'substantial' part of another person's work although we also learnt that 'substantial' is not legally defined but will vary from one situation to another. This is equally true when using websites but poses even more difficulties. It is hard enough to decide what is a substantial part of a book or magazine article but websites are much more complicated and often contain lots of bits and pieces of information, sound and video as well as maps, pictures and other graphics. Whether you are allowed to take less than a substantial part of the whole lot or just of each piece will not be easy to decide. In any case, if you look back to Monday where we saw that databases are a separate class, some websites also qualify for this definition, so the whole area is a minefield of untried law. As in all minefields, tread carefully.

What harm would my use of the work do? There are lots of ways that the use of another person's website might do harm, some of them far from obvious at first glance. We have already looked at using material from a website for competitive or similar reasons but there are other areas to think about too. For example:

- taking away income by making a competing product
- taking away income by not paying for use
- misleading users
- spoiling the reputation of the owner.

If you copy some distinctive features of someone's website and use them to create your own product, you may be in competition with the original owner. By using their creative work, you not only save yourself time and effort, you also go into competition with them using their own materials. This could be judged a very serious infringement in a court.

If you want to use someone's website material with safety, it is best to ask their permission. When you do this, you may find they make a charge or impose certain conditions (see Licences tomorrow). This is normal commercial practice, so failure to seek permission means that the owner has lost out on some hard cash. So you may not only be competing with them, but also depriving them of legitimate revenue.

There is also a danger of misleading users if you use someone else's work and put your name on it. The user thinks you made it, when it actually came from someone else. It could also be of less quality than the original thus denting the reputation of the actual owner. Even if all you do is take some text that they wrote and put it into your own magazine article to save you the effort of writing it all over again, they may still see this as damaging their academic or moral standing as well as their economic rights.

Has the owner specified what I can or can't do? Although this may seem a fairly obvious question, it is worth repeating. If the owner has said 'Anything may be done with this work' then you can literally do anything with it. But if the owner has said 'This work may be used only for non-commercial purposes' then that is a condition and must be complied with. But we shall deal with this in more detail tomorrow.

The composer Jean-Michel Jarre put all his music on the web so that people could experiment with changing it in different ways. However, this could not be used subsequently for commercial recordings. Ordnance Survey allow users to download their maps from the web, even for inclusion in users' own websites, but limits on the number you can use are set.

Intranets

Use of material on intranets is much the same as websites, both in terms of making an intranet site and using one. However, one or two specific notes need to be made about intranets generally.

Creating an intranet
Again, there is no problem using material from within the organization or company, but other material must be used in exactly the same way as when creating a website. Owners of copyright will not usually be sympathetic to the plea that the material was available only within the company and not to the general public. The reason for this is that if the material is thought so useful that it should be available company-wide, then it must have quite a high value to that company so why shouldn't they pay for it? Sometimes people infringe by putting something on a website which is much more widely available but which brings them little or no financial benefit. This is often seen by owners as less threatening than an intranet use.

Using an intranet site.
As access to intranets is usually limited to employees or users of an institution's services, they have the right to expect that all the material is 'clean' from a copyright point of view and they can do whatever is necessary with it. Users of intranets are far less conscious of copyright limits than website users for this reason. Therefore, it is important that managers make

sure that all materials on their intranets are cleared for use and do not mislead users into thinking they can do things which they cannot.

Email

Emails are slippery things – here one minute and gone the next. But they are still eligible for the same copyright protection as anything else, provided they fulfill the basic criteria. And this is where common sense is necessary. On Sunday we learnt that two of the conditions for copyright are being fixed and being original. Many email messages fail the second test but not usually the first:

> Joe: Are you coming to the pub tonight?
> Mary: Yes, which pub?
> Joe: Royal Dog & Duck, 7 o'clock. OK?
> Mary: OK

Both then delete the message.

None of this is 'original' (not even the name of the pub) but commonplace chit-chat. A long email, detailing company accounts or policy, which is stored in a folder by the recipient, would certainly qualify and must be treated just like anything else. Once its eligibility for copyright is established, the usual rules apply in all respects. However, one interesting question remains: if you send the same message simultaneously to 30 people, do you make 30 copies or do you sent 30 simultaneous transmissions? Nobody knows.

Summary

We have learnt that websites, intranets and emails are essentially the same as other copyright works. Websites need particular attention. When creating one it is important to remember the basic rules if you use someone else's materials and the potential harm you could cause them if you do. It is also important to protect your own website properly. There is a great temptation to say that it is so easy to download or copy from the net that it must be OK to do so but this is far from true. If you are using the net, also be careful that the rights of owners are respected and be aware of the potential economic significance of using other materials, especially for commercial, advertising or promotional use. Intranets are often seen as more of a threat to owners than open websites because of their economic value. Emails are deceptive in their temporary and often insignificant nature but have just as much right to protection as anything else if they are of significant size or content.

Some of the problems we identified today can be solved through agreements with owners in the form of contracts and licences and we shall learn more about those tomorrow.

Licences and liability

Yesterday we learnt something about the electronic world and how it is important to protect your own property and yet be able to use someone else's within the law. A lot of what we learnt hinged on the idea of the owner giving some kind of permission. Today we are going to explore some of the different ways permission can be given or obtained and then take a look at who is liable for what in copyright matters.

Licences or contracts?

Quite often these two terms are used as if they mean the same thing. In reality they are quite different as we shall see. A *licence* (in the US spelled license) is a document or some other mechanism which gives you official permission to do something. A *contract* is a formal agreement between all the parties concerned. It needs the agreement of all those taking part and must involve the exchange of money or goods. On the other hand, a licence can be a one-way device, giving someone, or a specified group, permission to do something which they might want to do (or might not). These are not legal definitions but general guidance for the sake of trying to sort them out for general copyright purposes. Sometimes the two terms can be misleading: for example, 'Made under licence' means that the company making the lawnmowers or brewing the beer have actually agreed terms with the owner of the patent or trademark to be able to do this in return for a payment. This is really a contract.

Licences

Licences can take many forms and have benefits and drawbacks for both the owner (licensor) and user (licensee). These have to be weighed up very carefully especially if your company owns copyright and wants to license it to other people.

Broadly speaking, licences divide into several different types:

- totally open and gratuitous
- very general in terms of who can do what
- very general in terms of what cannot be done
- specific in terms of who can do what
- specific in terms of what cannot be done
- based on highly detailed terms and conditions.

Remember that copyright is a property right. The owner is free to decide what will be allowed and what will not.

As the owner of copyright material, you may have quite a complex set of views about how you are prepared to allow your property to be used. One of the problems of copyright is that the law gives you a bundle of rights whether you want them or not and the only way to straighten this out is by some kind of licence. This highlights a very important point in any licensing generally, namely that owners may set whatever terms and conditions they wish for the use of their own property.

A research company produces a detailed study of the dangers of mobile phones to health. The report is expensive and the company would not want it copied at all. The same company produces a short leaflet outlining the potential dangers for the benefit of the general public. They actually want this to be copied so that it is distributed as widely as possible. The company will fiercely defend its rights in the report but willingly allow the leaflet to be copied. So the report will be marked with the usual warnings about copying whilst the leaflet might say 'this may be freely copied and distributed.'

We have just seen that there are different types of licence and the example of a mobile phone company showed two of them. In one case there is no licence at all because the company wants to control the material completely and the other you are absolutely free to do whatever you like. Most completely free licences still have certain conditions attached to them so that the material cannot be used for commercial purposes or republished in a different form. The owner usually expects their name to be included in it whenever it is used or quoted. Quite often educational publishers will allow their material to be copied for classroom use but not to be included in study packs or reformatted to form other materials in different institutions.

Managing licences
If your organization owns the copyright in something, they may wish to licence it to different people in different ways. In the same way, if you wish to use copyright material you may want a licence to do this. There is an increasing tendency throughout the world, not just in the UK, to develop licensing agencies which act on behalf of a large number of owners and users. These agencies issue standard licences

which anybody can take out. They collect royalties from those using copyright material and distribute these to the owners. This usually requires some sort of statistical sampling to find out what is copied or used most often and how the money shall be distributed. In the UK there are an increasing number of licensing agencies and the addresses of the more important ones appear at the end of this chapter. These deal with:

- texts
- artistic works such as slides
- newspapers
- church music
- broadcasts (for education)
- performances.

The Copyright Licensing Agency acts on behalf of most publishers of books and magazines and will license schools, government departments, universities and commercial companies to make paper copies within strict limits. This means that much more copying than was previously possible can be done without a great deal of bureaucracy but, of course, in return for payments. The Performing Rights Society (PRS) similarly licenses the performance of music in public places. If your organization has a social club or puts on concerts or events using any form of music, you will almost certainly need a licence from the PRS. For education there is an Educational Recording Agency Licence (but not for commercial companies) and the Newspaper Licensing Agency behaves similarly to the Copyright Licensing Agency in licensing the use of the typography (in other words, the print of newspapers but not necessarily their contents). All of these agencies (and these are only the main ones) are also very active in pursuing people who infringe copyright and taking legal action against them.

Implied licences

Occasionally there are situations where no licence actually exists but the circumstances of using something make it fairly clear that the owner must allow copying. For example, if you buy a piece of software for your PC, the very act of loading it makes a copy. In the same way, viewing something on the screen also makes a further copy. As you cannot use the material without doing these technical actions there is considered to be an implied licence that you may make those copies for these purposes.

Using licensed material

Once an organization acts under any form of licence it is important that it sticks to the terms of the licence. If it is one of those where the owner has given permission without needing to enter into an agreement, those conditions must be observed. For example, a lot of government material such as Acts of Parliament may now be downloaded, copied, republished and included in other works without any formal permission. However, the text must not be changed in any way. If this is done without making it clear to the user, this will be an infringement of Crown Copyright, even though no actual agreement has been entered into. The company would have agreed to the terms of the licence which HMSO grants. Where a proper written licence exists, again the terms must be adhered to strictly.

A good example of this is the railway timetable where Rail Track allow you to view, download and copy the train times for your own use but set out a whole page of restrictions on how the material may be used. You are prevented from showing, playing or performing the work. I wonder when anybody last performed the railway timetable?

However it is a good example of a very detailed licence granted without the user having to take any specific action. If you do anything other than the things these conditions allow, you would still infringe copyright (but see later on about special exemptions).

Sometimes owners are quite happy to allow works to be widely copied and used because it is impossible to control, but set the price accordingly.

Recently, a piece of software was launched to help teachers write reports on pupils. It has all the necessary forms and a large number of prepared comments which can be used and modified for each child's report. However the price of this software is set at several hundred pounds on the assumption that it may be copied for anything from two to 200 teachers depending on the size of the school. But the owner is not concerned about the number of copies made because these have been estimated and the price set accordingly.

Licences and exceptions

As we saw on Wednesday, there are a number of exceptions to copyright to enable people to use material without having to seek permission. As these are not statutory rights but privileges, users have to be very careful to make sure that any licence which they sign or agree to does not deny them these privileges. There is an increasing tendency for owners to take the attitude of 'never mind the exceptions, let's agree on our own terms'. This may be OK but at the same time it may deprive you of privileges which Parliament wanted you to have. Therefore always try to keep the privileges given to users.

Agreeing to licences

It is fairly clear that there are lots of ways in which you can agree to the terms of a licence. The easiest one is simply to use the material you want in the way that the owner has stipulated. These conditions have to be read in conjunction with the exceptions which you may enjoy, but if you stray outside these conditions you will be just as likely to infringe as anybody else. Stick to both of these sets of rules and you will be OK. Other licences may require you to take some action to show you agree. For example to click on the square or icon on a website to indicate you agree is a fairly common practice these days. If you decline to click, you are usually denied access to the material you want. The licences issued by the licensing agencies just described usually include some form of indemnity. This means that, provided the user sticks to the conditions of the licence, the owners can't take action against them. If they do, the Licensing Agency usually picks up the case and sees it through the courts on behalf of the user. The other side of this is that the conditions must be strictly observed.

It is also likely that owners would take action against a company, rather than against an individual employee. Individual employees do not have much economic power to pay large sums in damages, unlike their employers. Even so, systematic and deliberate infringement would probably need to be demonstrated. Where an infringement takes place on a piece of equipment provided for general public use (such as in academic or public libraries), the law is clear that the person doing the copying is responsible and not the organization that owns and provides the copying machine. By analogy, this would be true of people using public Internet access equipment and subsequently infringing material from individual web sites. On the other hand, if somebody who has general supervision of the equipment is aware that systematic infringement is taking place, they probably have a duty as a professional person and as a general citizen to draw this to the attention of the user. If this fails, it is quite legitimate to point out that equipment is provided for proper legal use and not for abuse and under these terms you could stop somebody using the equipment in the future.

Shrink wrap licences

These are usually used for software, CD-ROMs and other electronic materials. The idea behind this is that if you break the seal of the packaging this shows you have agreed to the licence. However a general view is that if this licence is not visible through the wrapping then it cannot be binding as you did not know the terms to which you were supposed to agree. This has never been tested in court but is a general opinion. Where the terms of a licence seem utterly unreasonable, it is possible to appeal to the copyright tribunal but this is a long, complicated and very expensive process.

Contracts

As already stated today, a contract involves the exchange of goods and money or monies worth. It must be agreed by both parties and must be in writing as this is a requirement

for acquiring rights in copyright material. Agreements with
people over a pint in the bar won't stand up in court in this
case. As owner of copyright material, your organization may
wish to enter into fairly complex and detailed contracts about
the exploitation of it. Contracts will deal with a whole range
of issues including the following:

- what can be done
- in what format it can be done
- where it can be done
- how long it can be done for
- what happens at the end of the term of the contract
- particular conditions.

Let's say your company produces a detailed study of the
history and development of a particular piece of machinery.
This development includes several well-known figures in
your particular specialized area. The company then decides
to publish this because it is of wide and general interest. But
as the company is not a publishing firm itself, it may
approach a traditional publisher to do this. The company
may then decide any or all of the following. They may grant
the publisher all and every right in the work now and in the
future and in every form now existing or invented at some
later time. This is called an Assignment of Rights and means
that the company has no further interest in the work, having
handed all of this over to the publishing firm, hopefully in
return for a reasonable sum of money. A publisher can then
get on with doing whatever he wants with the book and the
firm has got its money and no further worries about it.
However, a senior executive may see rather more benefits in
retaining some of the rights and a variety of options
considered.

Liability

People often ask who is liable if copyright is infringed. In circumstances where copying is done by an individual for their own use and it is infringing, obviously they are responsible and action would be taken against them. However, going to court is a very expensive matter and owners are usually seeking damages so cases against isolated individuals are rare because they are simply not worth the investment of time and very expensive legal fees.

Internet service providers
An interesting question is who is liable if somebody mounts infringing copyright material on a website which is hosted by an internet service provider (ISP) who has no knowledge of this. The general principle, which also applies to areas such as libel and obscenity, is that if the ISP is merely a server provider and has no knowledge of the content of the material being provided, they are not liable. Liability rests with the person who created the original website. However, if the ISP is notified that the material is infringing (or libelous or obscene) and fails to remove it, they do become liable and can be taken to court for either criminal or civil proceedings.

Employees
Most infringement takes place in organizations such as companies or schools. In these cases, action would be taken against the institution as it is that which has the money and which probably authorized, or at least required, the copying to be done. A member of staff may ignore or be ignorant of the rules and regulations inside an institution and commit an infringement. The company would be held responsible for the overall actions of the staff member. The disciplinary

proceedings that followed would then be an internal matter. What if an employee uses the firm's photocopying machine to make infringing copies for their own private use? Well, the general view is that merely to provide equipment which could be used for an illegal purpose is not in itself an offence. If the company could not be expected to know of the activities of the employee, they cannot be held responsible in these circumstances. Nevertheless, clear guidelines for staff about private use of equipment should always be made available.

Gross infringement

Where anybody blatantly infringes the copyright of another person either by publishing a work, making multiple copies or actually using a work to create a sound recording or a film, it is certain that the copyright owner would take swift and extensive legal action. The first step for the owner would be to seek a court injunction to stop the work being distributed or published any further and then proceedings would start to recover damages which might be calculated both in terms of the amount of money the infringing person had made out of the owner's property and also the amount of money the owner had lost. Damages can be extensive and costs are often awarded against infringing organizations in this situation.

One example of gross infringement is where a copy shop made 300 copies of a management text book which was still in print and easily available from local bookshops.

Minor infringements

Where a minor infringement occurs, such as making two
copies of something for somebody or copying more of a
document than the owner considers reasonable, it is unlikely
that the owner would take the infringer to court unless it was
considered that this was really symptomatic of something
much greater going on within a company. Taking legal action
against copyright infringers is an expensive business and the
owner has to demonstrate that there was real economic or
other damage. It may be that if action was taken, it would be
to show that a licence should be taken out from one of the
agencies mentioned earlier. However, the most likely path
an owner would take would be to send a formal letter from a
solicitor pointing out that infringing copies had been made
and that the company should tighten up its procedures and
regulations. Whilst everybody should respect copyright,
nobody should become paranoid about very minor offences.
This applies to both owners and users.

A very long time ago, a judge in a copyright case said
that although owners of land have aerial rights, if an
owner took action against a balloonist because they
happen to fly over his field, the court would not even
entertain hearing the complaint.

Infringements of licences and contracts

Where a licence or contract is in place and an infringement
occurs, it is likely that the owner will take some action. In the
case of licences, it will depend on how much damage has
been done to the owner and how well the user understood

the licence that had been granted. The courts tend to interpret licences very narrowly so that broad and sloppy language does not actually catch people out. On the other hand, the terms of a contract, if it is properly drawn up, will be seen as binding both by the actual language used and the general interpretation of it. In both of these cases, it is unlikely that a case would be brought to court before the extended discussion had taken place between the owner and the user to find out what has happened and to try to come to some sort of settlement. This is of economic and political benefit to both parties as it makes the licensing or contract process much more desirable. However, in the final event a serious infringement would be taken to court.

Penalties

In most instances, copyright is a matter of civil law. The usual procedure for infringement would be a solicitor's letter, followed by a court injunction if the copying continued. If it still continued a case would be brought to court. In some cases, the court case is the first step, depending on the size and type of infringement that is going on. The courts would then award damages which can be calculated in various complex ways. They can include both the benefits to the infringer as well as the loss of income to the original owner and, therefore, can be very high.

For example, a well known shop identified a painting which it thought would look very nice on some mugs. The painting was bought and transferred to the mugs which were then put on sale. None of this was done with the owner's permission. The painter then saw the mugs and took legal action. This resulted in damages of about £20,000 and legal costs of a further £25,000 plus the destruction of all the mugs which had been manufactured.

Summary

We have learnt today that licences, contracts and liability are a crucial area in copyright management for both the owner and the user. Licences have a particular use in that they do not require individual contracts to be drawn up but a relationship is established between the owner and the user. They can simply be available for everybody to agree in general terms. Contracts are much more detailed and binding but will always involve the exchange of money and goods to the mutual benefit of everybody concerned, whereas a licence may bring no obvious benefits to the owner. In either case, proper advice should be sought if the value of the material being licensed or contracted out is of significance to the owning company. In the same way, somebody wishing to exploit copyright material should make sure the contract grants them all the rights they need to carry out their business. Organizations need to be aware that they may be liable for infringement done by members of their staff who are unlikely to be taken to court as individuals but may be subject to disciplinary procedures internally. Internet service providers need to be aware that if and when they are notified of material which should not be on their servers, they must remove this promptly or also face the possibility of court proceedings.

Useful addresses

Authors' Licensing &
Collecting Society (ALCS)
Marlborough Court
14–18 Holborn
London EC1N 2LE
Tel 0207 395 0600
Fax 0207 395 0660
Email alcs@alcs.co.uk
Website
http://www.alcs.co.uk
[very useful for tracking down authors and owners]

British Copyright Council
29–33 Berners Street
London W1V 4AA
Tel 020 7306 4464
Fax 020 7306 4740
Email
British.copyright.council
@dial.pipex.com
[Represents owners' interests]

Copyright Licensing Agency
90 Tottenham Court Road
London W1P 9HE
Tel 020 7436 5931
Fax 020 7436 3986
Email cla@cla.co.uk

Website
http://www.cla.co.uk

Design and Artists
Copyright Society
Parchment House
13 Northburgh Street
London EC1V 0AH
Tel 020 7336 8811
Fax 020 7336 8822
www.dacs.co.uk

HMSO Copyright Section
St Clements
Colegate
Norwich NR3 1BQ
Tel 01603 521000
Fax 01603 723000
Website
http://www.hmso.gov.uk

Newspaper Licensing
Agency
Lonsdale Gate
Lonsdale Gardens
Tunbridge Wells
Kent TN1 1NL
Tel 01892 525273
Fax 01892 525275
Email copy@nla.co.uk
Website
http://www.nla.co.uk

Copyright Branch
Ordnance Survey
Romsey Road
Maybush
Southampton SO9 4DH
Tel 01703 792706
Fax 01703 792535
www.ordsvy.gov.uk

Performing Rights Society
29/33 Berners Street
London W1P 4AA
Tel 020 7306 064
Fax 020 7306 4740
www.prs.co.uk

A corporate policy

So far this week we have learnt a great deal about copyright and in the last chapter we explored the ways in which material can be exploited both by owners and users. We now need to think what this means in terms of a corporate policy for an organization.

Protecting and exploiting what you own

Nearly every organization generates material which is copyright. Although a lot of it may seem trivial or unimportant at the time, it may later assume considerable significance for a company or institution and actually start to attract real monetary value. Managers need to be sharply aware of those areas where copyright material may be created. Steps need to be taken to make sure staff are aware of the economic value of what they create and also the rights the company or organization has over this material. A number of areas need to be examined quite carefully to make sure that as much protection as possible is being given to the organization's assets. Areas on which it is worth focusing include:

- marketing
- publicity and public relations
- research and development
- training
- administration
- student work.

Marketing

Marketing departments (which may include publicity) generate a huge amount of material. This may be text of various kinds, photographs, logos or slogans. A very large amount of this material will be copyright and steps should be taken to make sure that staff are aware of this and it is properly protected. If somebody else is found using similar or the same material, action should be taken swiftly to protect the company's marketing and products. Keep a sharp eye open for companies using your material in comparative advertising, for example. Make sure that any logos are registered as trade or service marks where possible. At the same time, make sure the contracts which are issued to any outside design or advertising companies give your organization all the rights it needs over that material to use it both now and in the future. Always remember that new media are always being developed and so you will want to make sure you have got the maximum amount of rights over everything you have commissioned.

Publicity and public relations

This is in many ways similar to marketing but it may focus more on texts and images such as photographs and will attract a certain number of letters from customers. Such letters may be useful for publicity purposes, but make sure the writer of the letter agrees to this before it is used. You may own any letters that customers send you, but you do not own the copyright in them.

Research and development

Research and development (R&D) staff will generate a huge amount of copyright material (as well as other products which may be suitable for patents or trademarks). Any

technical reports that they write or papers that they prepare
for magazines or give at conferences will be the property of
the organization. This should be made clear to anybody who
wants to publish this material and suitable licences issued for
its use. Even if a report is put up on a website, the ownership
should be clearly indicated and a statement made about what
use can and cannot be made of it. Again, any R&D work
which is contracted out should be tightly controlled by
contracts to ensure that the organization obtains all the rights
from those doing the research work.

NO, I DON'T OWN THE RIGHTS TO
THE TEA ROUND!

Training section
Many organizations have training sections of various kinds.
These often generate a great deal of internal material ranging
from printed leaflets and work books through to videos, web
sites and multi-media productions. All this material is
copyright and, again, should be carefully protected. Where it
might be supplied to people outside the organization, the
ownership of the copyright and conditions of use should be
clearly stated. On a video, for example, this should be the
first thing that the user sees even before the title is displayed.

We have already discussed different ways of showing
ownership and permission to use web sites.

Administration
Although administration departments rarely generate
copyright material themselves, they may be the department
responsible for issuing or agreeing to contracts and licences
with outside bodies. Staff in this area should be made aware
of the importance of controlling the copyright element of any
contract or licence. It is easy for this important element to be
overlooked in the wealth of detail, especially if the contract is
complex or involves mostly manufacturing processes.

Using copyright material

There are a number of departments who may use copyright
material. Some of these will be the same as those creating it,
but others will only be users. These include:

- library and information services
- marketing and publicity
- research and development
- training
- social activities
- administration
- students.

Library and information services
Where an organization has a library or information service
the staff need to be aware of the special regulations relating
to libraries, as described on Wednesday. The library may
contain a self-service photocopying machine and users
should be aware of the limitations under which this can be

used (as we discussed on Wednesday). When the library offers a copying service on behalf of users, the necessary declaration forms need to be in place. The library is often seen as somewhere that may have information about copyright and a suitable manual or textbook on copyright should be included in the library collection.

Marketing and publicity
Marketing and publicity staff are often very enthusiastic and can get carried away with their ideas. They need to be fully aware of the danger of using material which has already been produced by somebody else. Using quotations from published books or poems, photographs, clips from radio or TV programmes and pieces of information from other people's websites will all probably be infringements. Even a small quotation used for marketing purposes could lead to legal action because the owner may see your organization benefiting commercially from the use of the quotation. Similarly, slogans and logos which are similar to those used by other organizations need to be avoided or checked with the Trademark Department of the Patent Office.

Research and development
Although there is no problem with reading material produced by somebody else and using this as the basis for your own ideas, R&D staff need to be aware that they cannot merely take large chunks of other peoples' papers and incorporate them in their own reports or conference presentations. They also need to consider carefully the use of existing designs when designing a new product as this could be an infringement of copyright as well as the rights of the owner in the design itself. Design Right is a quite separate right, as we discussed on Monday. Copying, even for an internal report,

will be seen as an infringement. Again, owners will see the use of even small parts of text as of benefit to your organization and may consider it worth taking legal action.

Training

There is a great temptation for people working in training to use all sorts of material to build up their courses and get the message across. Clear guidelines for trainers should be drawn up for the following areas at least:

- multiple copying of articles from magazines and books
- reproducing diagrams or pictures from books and magazines for OHP or powerpoint presentations
- using clips from radio and TV programmes
- downloading website material
- multiple copying of commercial published worksheets.

Training is an area of particular sensitivity for owners since much of this can be licensed by them at considerable profit and they would also see the benefit of training materials to a company or organization as particularly high as it enhances their commercial capabilities.

Social events

Does your organization have a social club or staff restaurant/canteen where music is played? If the answer is 'yes' then you need to make sure you have obtained the proper licences. If you put on events for outside organizations, such as pensioners' clubs or retired members then, again, you need to make sure you have the right licences and permissions. Even the use of copyright material in the staff pantomime or review will need licensing. A performance carried out in front of company employees is considered a public performance.

Administration

Administration departments do not see themselves as users of copyright material but they often need multiple copies of, say, magazine articles for discussion at board meetings or management seminars. These can be made only under licence so this area needs monitoring too.

Student work

Students who prepare work in schools, colleges and universities usually own the rights in what the produce. Unless they have signed an agreement when they enrolled, they will have the right to say how their work can be used. Copying pictures for promotional material, selling CDs of student music or using their written work to show how good the college is are all infringements. Where work has been produced by a student as part of their employment in a company, however, the company will own the rights. But it is important to check this out. Never make any assumptions about ownership.

Other departments

Of course, each organization is different and will arrange its departments according to its own needs. You may well be able to identify other areas which need special attention. If you have read this far, you ought to be able to work out which ones might need closer examination.

Keeping up-to-date

As we found out on Sunday, copyright is a constantly changing area. New laws, European directives, case law and technological developments all combine to make it a 'shifting sands' type of area. Therefore it is vital that somebody in an organization tries to keep as up-to-date as possible with various developments. A list of useful resources is given at the end of this book. Try not to be daunted by the detail. In most situations, all you need to do is be aware of the implications of a case or a new piece of law rather than analyzing the minute detail of what took place. If you do find a situation where detailed analysis is needed, it is best to seek advice from a specialist.

A copyright focal point

Experience shows that most people have little or no understanding of copyright and are very often cavalier about their approach to it. Therefore it is always a good idea for organizations to identify one person or department who will take responsibility for an issue such as copyright. This can then be a resource for the company in terms of information and guidance but could also take a proactive role in looking at developments in the company and identifying potential areas of copyright difficulty. There is nothing worse than developing a product or service only to be told later on that it is illegal and having to delete it or seriously modify it. This makes neither economic nor marketing sense. Just where such a focal point should be is for each organization to decide, but experience shows there should be one and it should be well known. Focal points can also take a role in educating staff in the basic principles set out in this book (but do not copy large chunks of it for training purposes!).

Your personal involvement

If you have found reading this book quite stimulating and interesting, you may be the right person to be a focal point in your organization. Although this can be a rather frightening prospect at first, it can also be extremely rewarding. This is a highly specialized but crucially important area for any organization, whether in the private or public sector. A reasonable understanding of the issues puts any individual in a key position to move the organization's strategy forward. It also provides an excellent basis for career development in a broader sense. Copyright specialists are few and far between, so why not get involved?

Summing up

Over the past week, we have explored a number of aspects of copyright and it may be worth reminding ourselves what we have actually learnt.

First, copyright is a property right and should be seen in the same way as any other sort of property. It gives the owner certain exclusive rights which are detailed in the law and also gives the owner the right to stop other people doing any of these actions without permission. We have identified who is the author (creator) of different types of work, what rights they enjoy and the way they determine how long copyright will last. We do have certain limited rights as individuals regardless of the property right which is largely concerned with economic value. We have gained some idea of how the law works and its complexities in terms of major legislation, statutory instrument, European directives and case law. To stop copyright becoming a total monopoly, the law sets out certain exceptions which can help users of copyright material without them needing to consult the owner. It is clear that these are very limited and should be exercised with care, but they exist and Parliament intended that copyright should not be an exclusive monopoly.

Finally

This little book is only an introduction to copyright and its main aim is to alert the reader to the problems rather than offer too many solutions. If it has helped organizations to identify areas where they should take action and improve their economic or commercial performance, it will have succeeded. If it helps to identify areas where there are problems in using material, it will also have succeeded. It gives a bird's eye view of a highly complex and dynamic area of law which is going to be of increasing importance to everybody in education, public service, commerce and industry, as well as our personal lives, in the future. Whether we are recording a TV programme at home, writing a poem, preparing a technical report, designing some marketing material or just a slide show for a kids' party, we still need to know about copyright. Some ways of finding out more are given in the bibliography and useful sources of information on the following pages.

Selected further sources of information

There are numerous legal textbooks on copyright. Most of them are intended for practising lawyers and can be confusing if you are trying to sort out a general issue. Any good library can provide a list for you. However, below are some useful books which you should find helpful.

Cornish, Graham P, *Copyright: interpreting the law for libraries, archives and information services*. 3rd revised edition. London, Library Association, 2001. ISBN 1 85604 409 2. Done in a 'question-and-answer' format for easy reference. Covers most basic issues in copyright.

Garnett, Kevin et al, *Copinger and Skone-James on copyright*. 14th edition, London: Sweet & Maxwell, 1999. (2 volumes). ISBN 0 421 589 108 (The Copyright Bible).

Henry, Michael. *Current copyright law*. London, Butterworths, 1998. ISBN 0 406N 896208. Gives the full text of the original Copyright Designs and Patents Act with all the amendments included in their correct place. This avoids the need to keep switching from one book to another. Very clear.

Wall, Raymond A, *Copyright made easier*. 3rd ed. London, Aslib, 2000. ISBN 0 85142 447 3. Covers all issues on a broad basis.

Aslib Guide to Copyright. London, Aslib, 1994+. An ongoing loose-leaf publication with regular updates. Available on subscription.

Several magazines cover UK and international developments. The more readable are:

Copyright World
European Intellectual Property Review
Current Law (lists recent copyright cases)

Useful websites include

www.intellectual-property.gov.uk
A website maintained by the Patent Office to give information on a wide range of Intellectual Property issues.

www.courtservice.go.uk
Gives official transcript of major cases. Searchable by subject.

www.bbc.co.uk/news
Surprisingly useful for latest news on copyright, especially in the media.